TECHNICAL ANALYSIS FOR FOREX DUMMIES

BY: JANE WOODBURN (PhD)

DISCLAIMER AND TERMS OF USE

Forex Trading has a large potential rewards but also carries potential risk. You must be aware of the risk and be willing to accept them in other to invest in the forex market.

Don't trade with money you can't afford to lose. The past performance of any trading system, strategy or methodology is not necessarily indicative of future results.

The beauty of this system is that 'you can never go broke trading it' Yes, I said so.

This work is the Intellectual property of Professor Jane Woodburn and cannot be reproduce in whatsoever way or form by any person/body/institution/website without proper permission. This is to avoid legal implications.

INTRODUCTION

"Technical Analysis for Dummies" affords us the opportunity to analyse the forex market using the information provided by the mt4/mt5 chart data. It is not dependent of the fundamentals/News information, so we are going to be using the wave structural analysis on 2 different trading strategies on the 4hours time frame. Also included is a Bonus trading strategy.

1. EXPANDED TRIANGLE TRADING SYSTEM:

This trading system is a simple trading strategy that makes use of head and shoulder to make "Expanded Triangle" market structure. See what extended triangle structure looks like in fig.1 below;

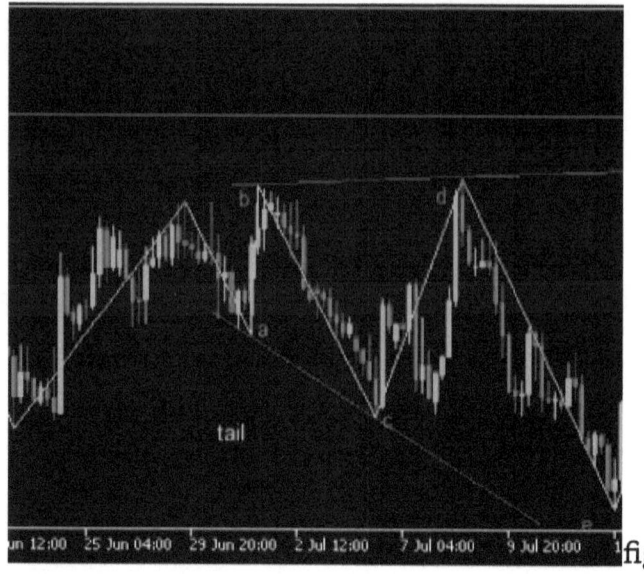
fig.1

I have been trading this strategy for the past 10years and I have not seen a reason not to continue because it so profitable and reliable so I decided to share. Mind you, this system works in any market condition and in any currency pair.

EXPANDED TRIANGLE MARKET STRUCTURE AND RULES;

The rules are very simple to follow too. You just need to;

    i)   Spot the head and shoulder market structure on the 4hr time frame as seen below.

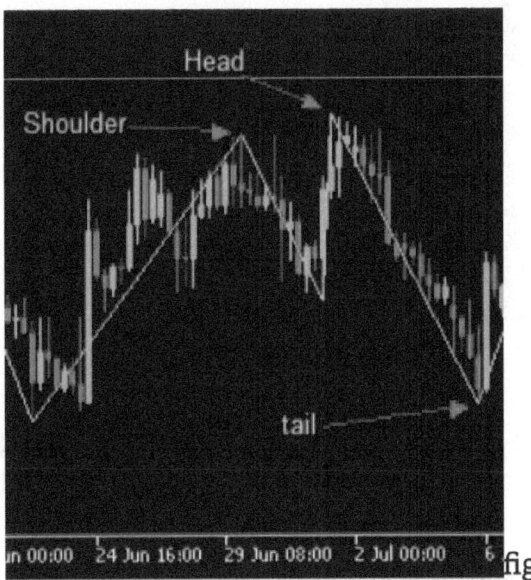

fig.2

ii) Allow price to test the Head line and tail line as can be seen below,

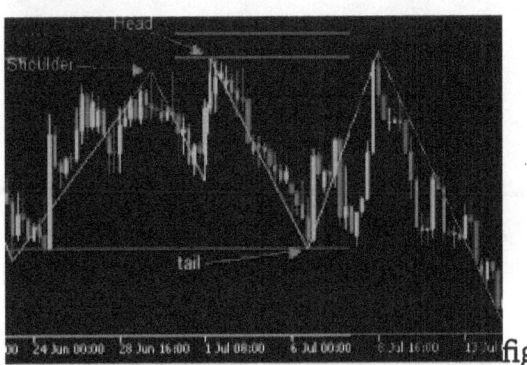

fig.3

iii) Wait for a swing and candle to emerge and close back into that broken tail line as can be seen below,

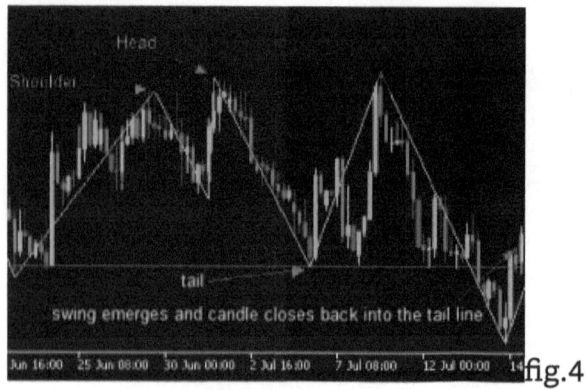

fig.4

iv) Once the above happens, use a pending limit order to place entry1 at that tail line and entry2 at 10pips to the recent swing peak.

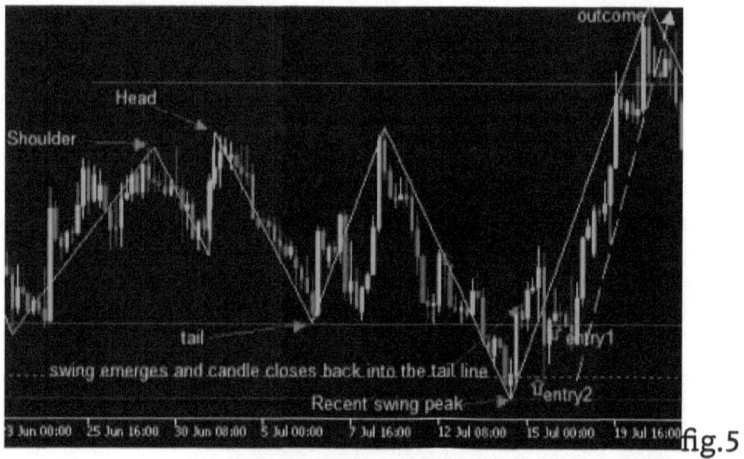

fig.5

v) Stop loss (SL) is place at 70pips behind that recent swing peak

vi) Take profit (TP) is from that head line peak level.

Let's see other examples of this extended triangle kind of market structure and how they played out in the figures below;

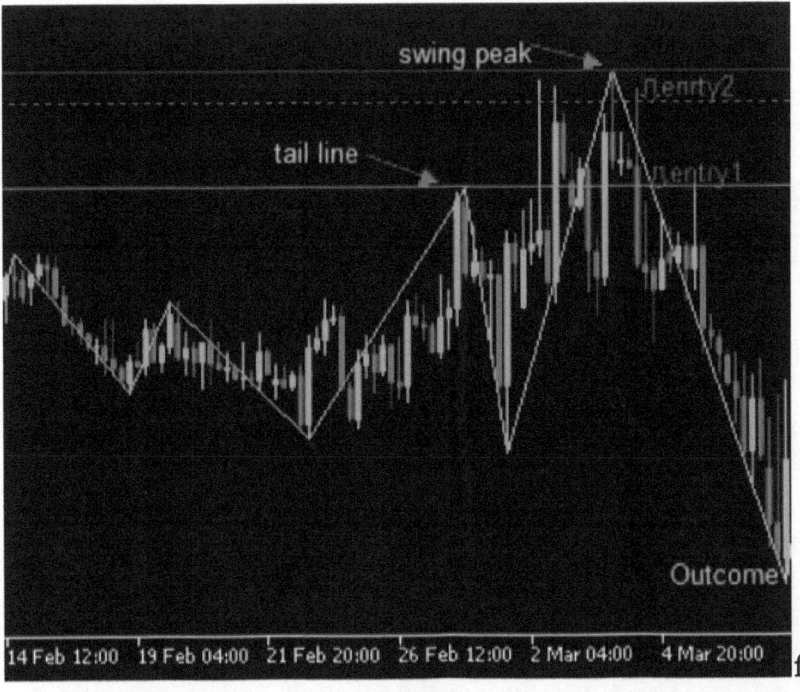

fig.6

fig.7

TECHNICAL ANALYSIS FOR FOREX DUMMIES

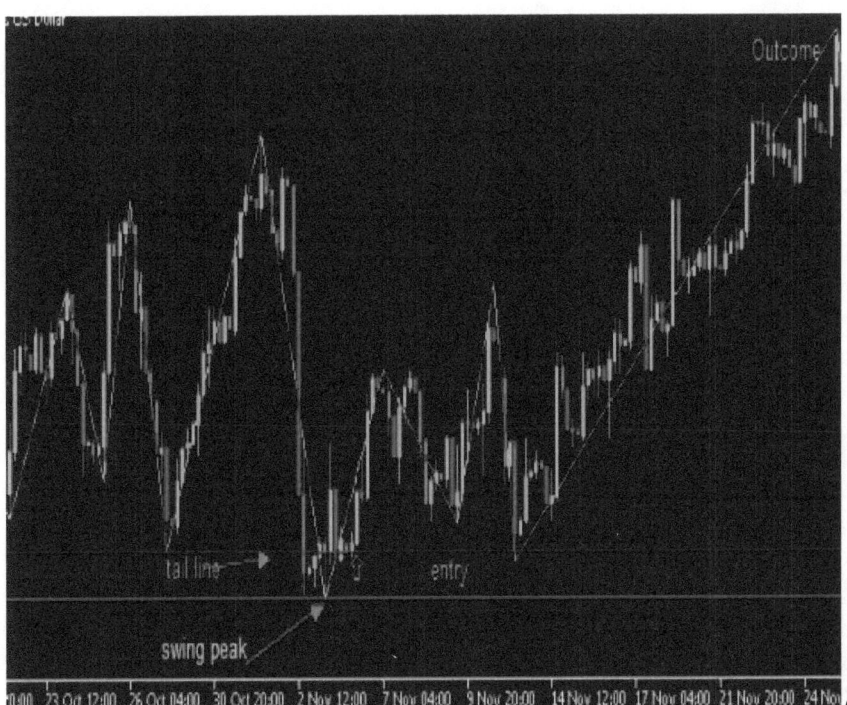

fig.8

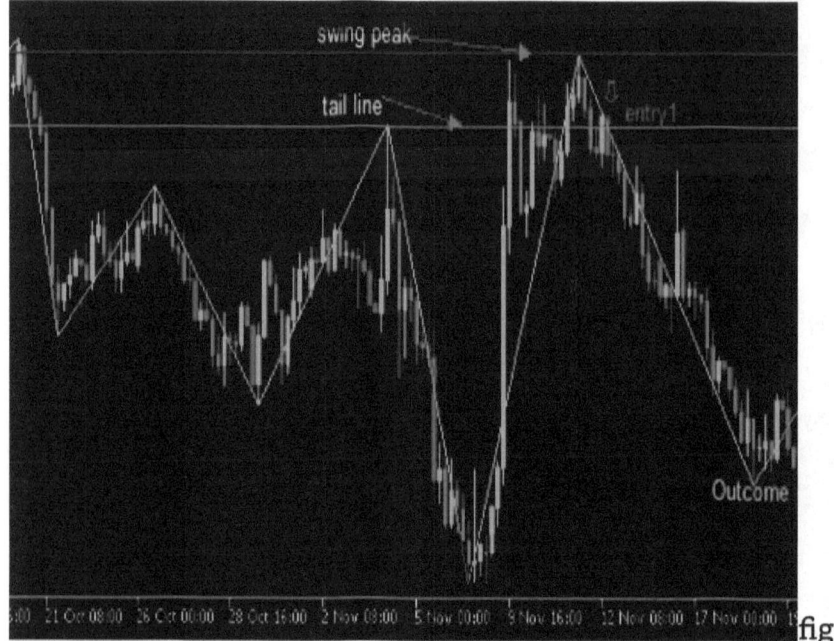
fig.9

TECHNICAL ANALYSIS FOR FOREX DUMMIES

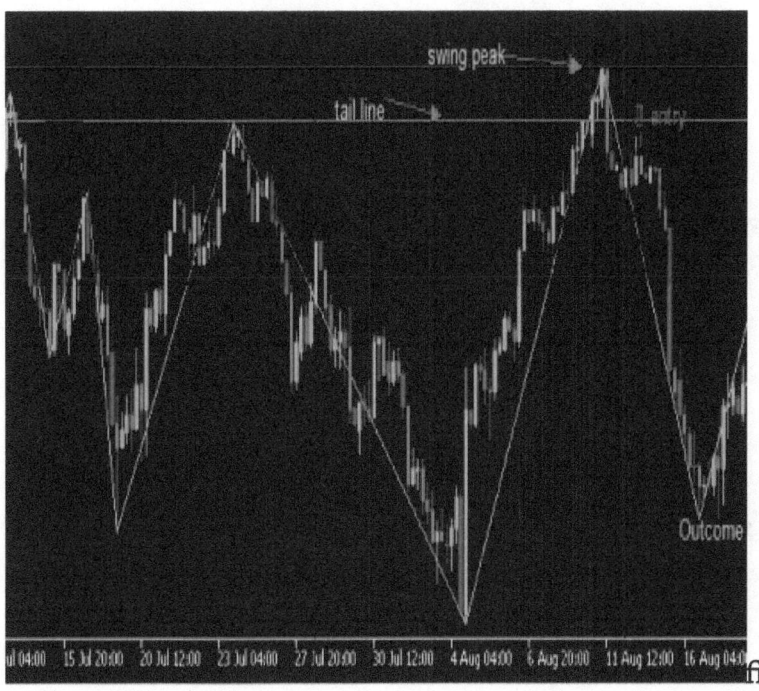

fig.10

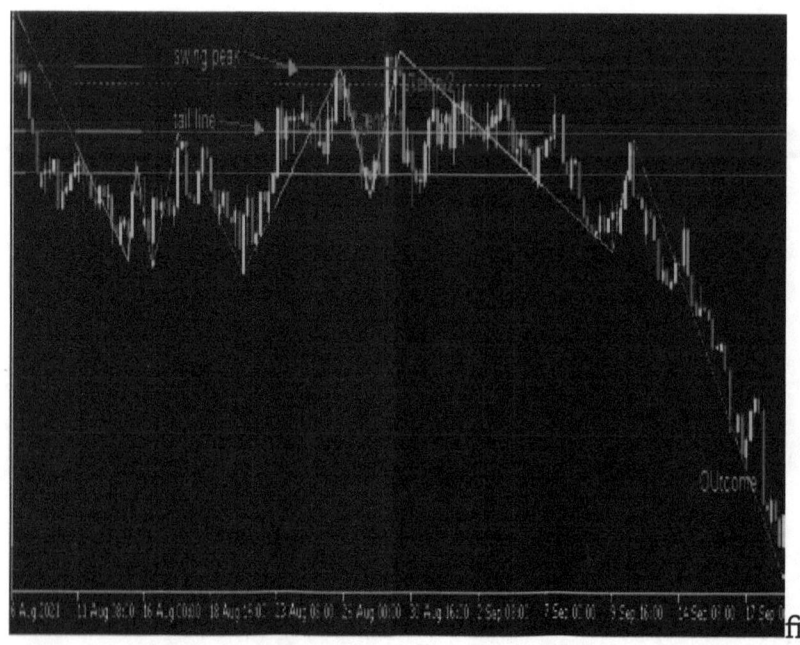

fig.11

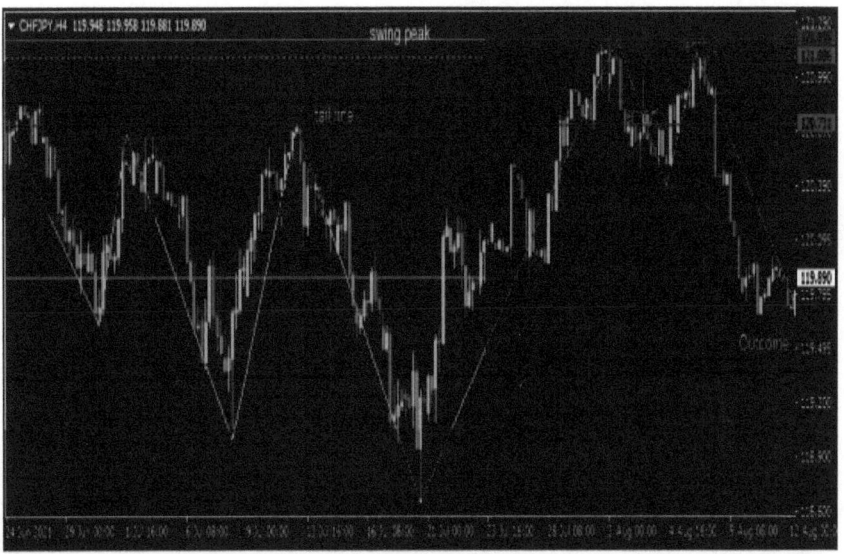

fig.12

2. THE 5 WAVES TREND LINE TRADING SYSTEM.

This is a trend continuation trading system. A market structure with an Overlapping /Non-overlapping impulsive 5 waves retrace in form of an ABC corrective wave structure that terminates around a support/resistance trend line is tipped to continue with the impulsive trend direction. Using the help of our default mt4/mt5 custom 'zigzag' indicator, Let's see what this structure looks like as it can be seen in between the two vertical lines in the chart fig.1, 2 & 3 shown below;

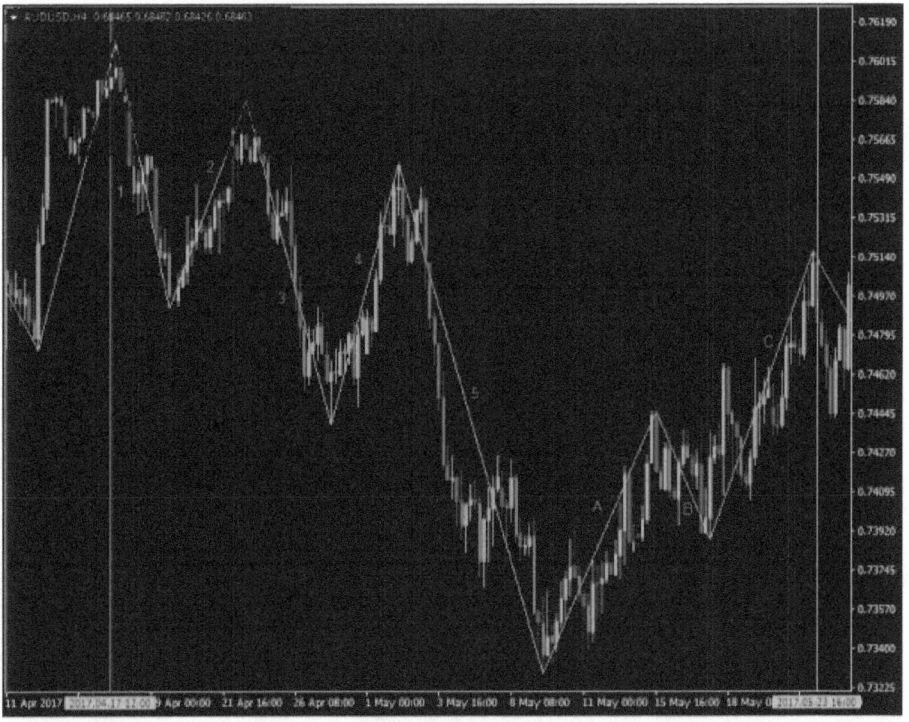

fig.13

BENJAMIN ZENERO

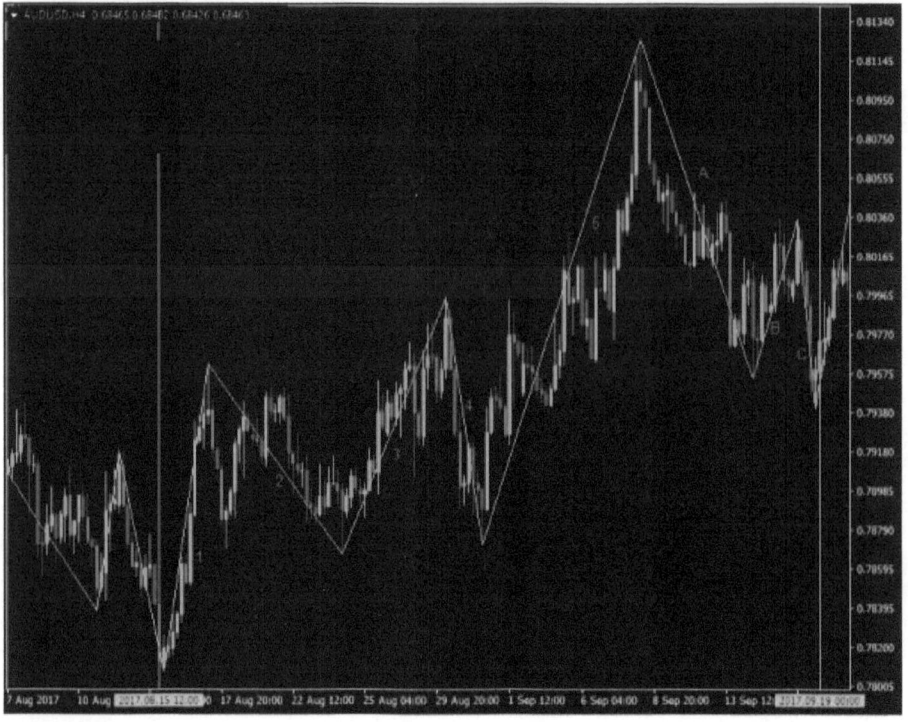

fig.14

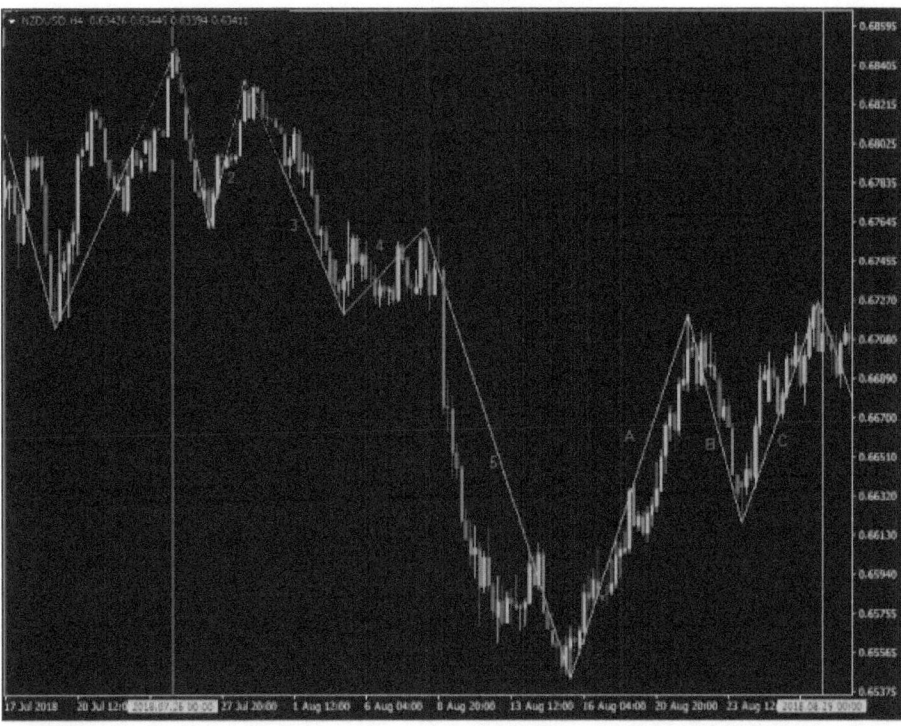

fig.15

RULES FOR TREND LINING THIS STRUCTURE, ENTRY, STOP LOSS AND TAKE PROFIT

- **The major rule in Trend lining** this kind of structure is to place your trend line connecting wave1 start point to the more relax peak. This can be either wave3 or wave5 start point. To do this, you have to make two trend lines; 1st one should connect wave1 start point to wave3 start point while the 2nd trend line should connect wave1 start point to wave 5 start point. Then look at both trend lines to choose the one that is more relax among the two (that is, the one price would get to last), that is the trend line we would work with. Delete the other one.

- Now that we have gotten our trend line, ensure that the wave A swing did **not touch** the trend line (even in its horizontal line intersection).

- Place your **Entry1** (0.01x1) using pending limit order whenever wave C price touches the trend line. **Entry2** (0.01x2) at 40pips from Entry1 price. (If entry2 was activated and price moves positively plus 50pips, close one entry2 and the entry one and move the other entry2 to BE).

- Stop Loss at **40pips from the wick of that candle that first break the trend line.**

- **Take Profit;** Place the mt4 Fibonacci Retracement indicator on the wave5. Then your take profit should be starting from 78.6% Fibonacci level. Deciding to hold the trade more than that level is at your discretion, just make sure you move you stop loss to break even to avoid converting your winner to a loser.

So let's see example with the chart on fig.4, 5, 6, 7, 8, 9 & 10

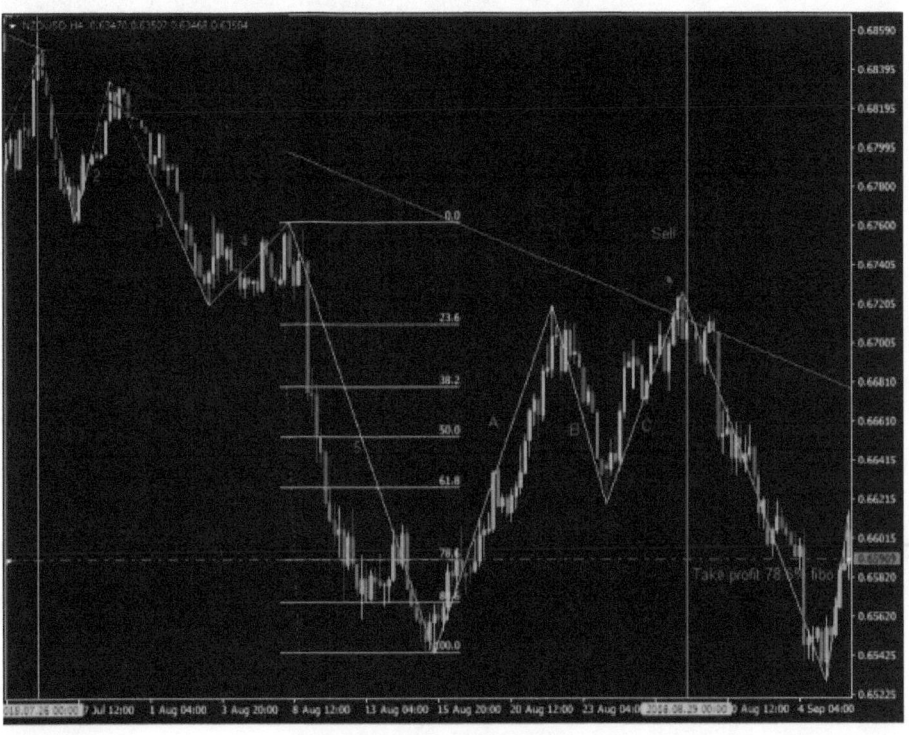

fig.16

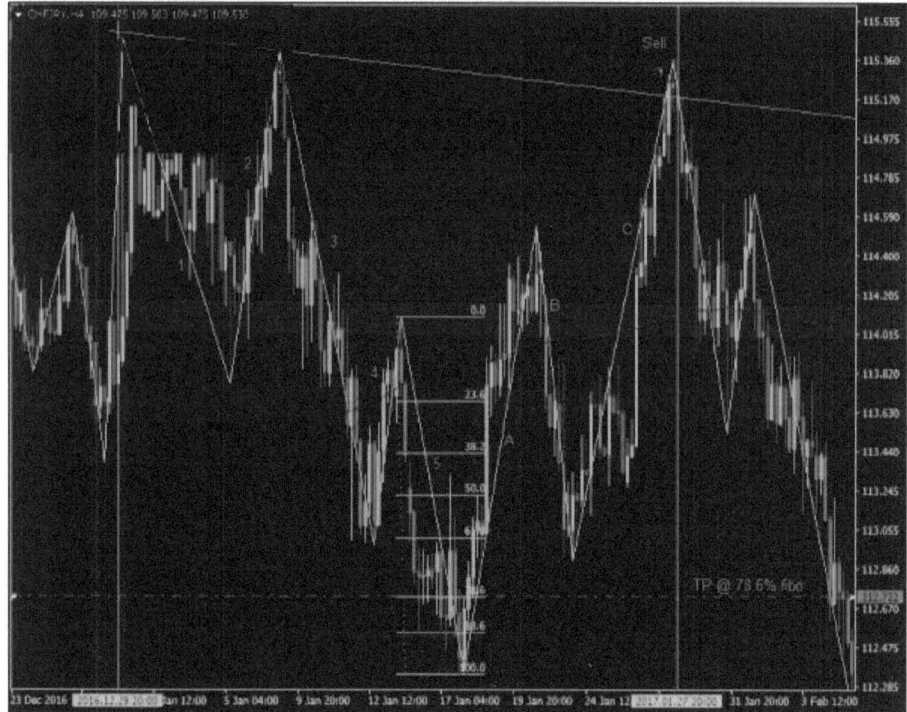
fig.17

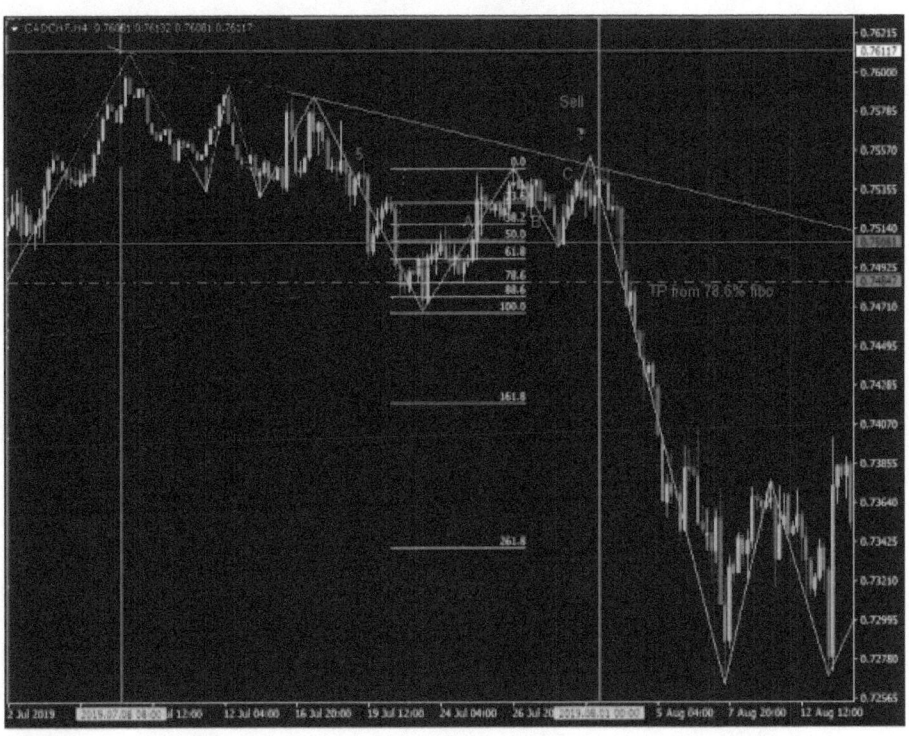

fig.18

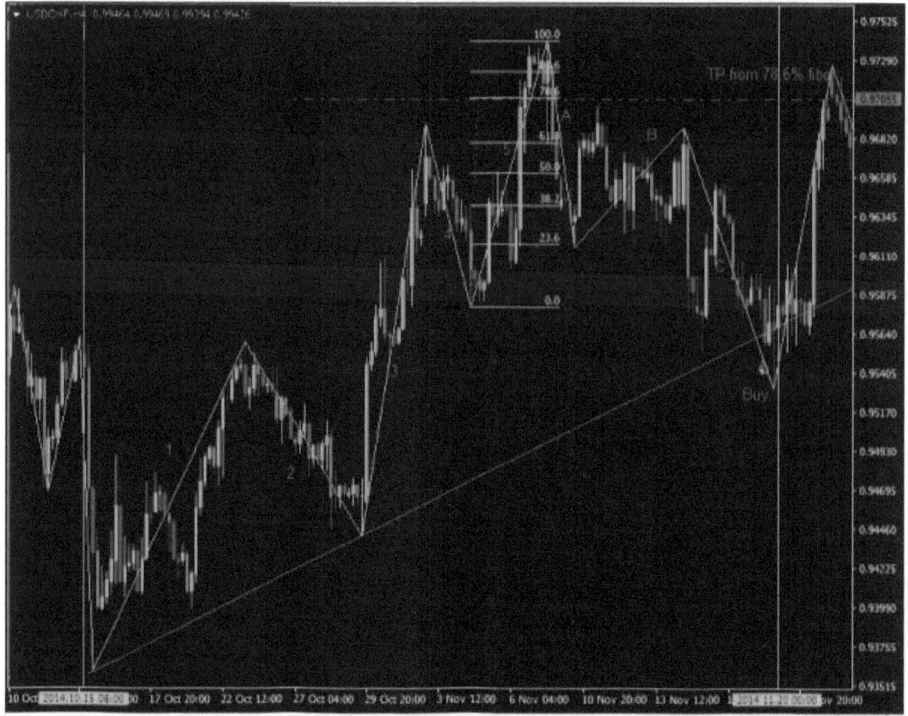

fig.19

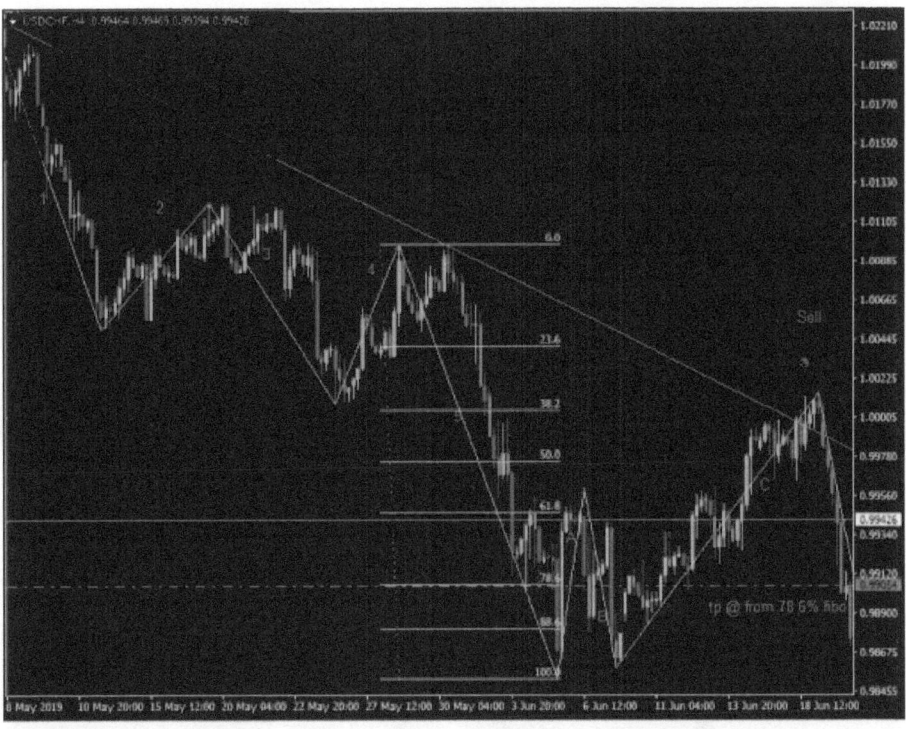

fig.20

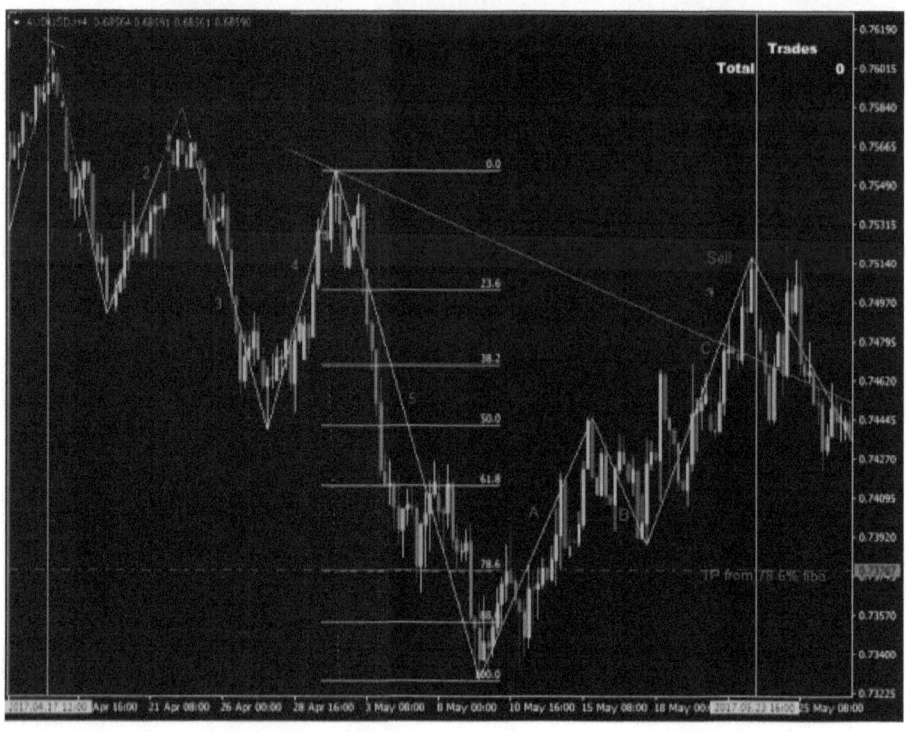

fig.21

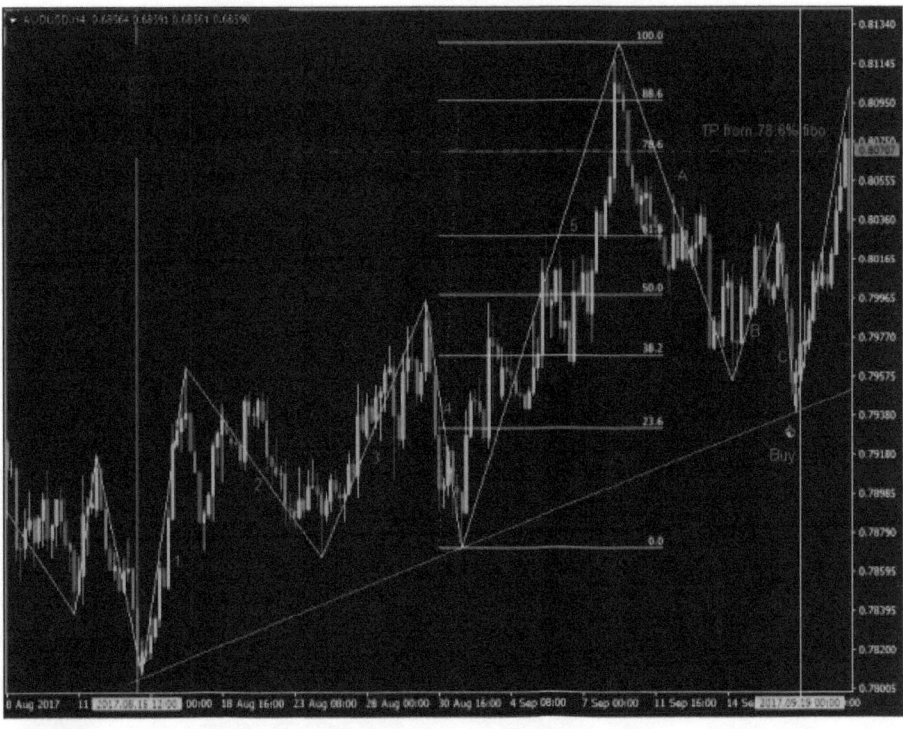

fig.22

BENJAMIN ZENERO

fig.23

BONUS TRADING SYSTEM:
For AudUsd only.

A bonus for the above technical analysis comes in a single wave (that may be from fresh swing or an initial abc...) plus an opposing immediate ABC whose wave-A did not touch the 61.8% fibo level before the emergence of wave-C.

Entry1a by placing a pending order @ 61.8% fibo level while Entry1b @ 78.6 fibo level. Stop loss @ 20pips behind the positive swing.

Move SL to BE once positive swing emerges but if this positive swing touches wave-B peak or breaks wave-AB TL, return the SL back to 5pips behind positive swing.

See example below

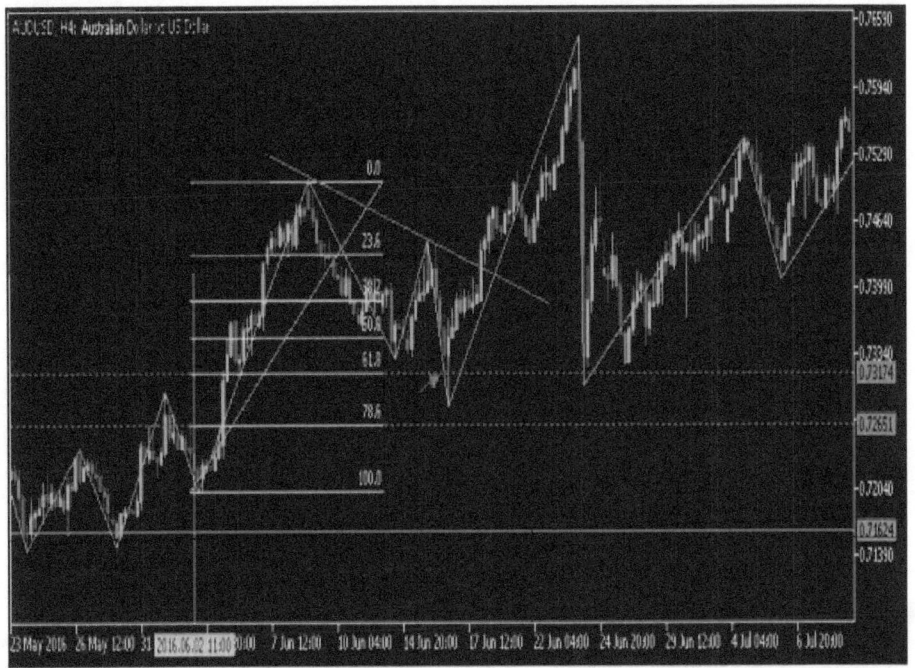

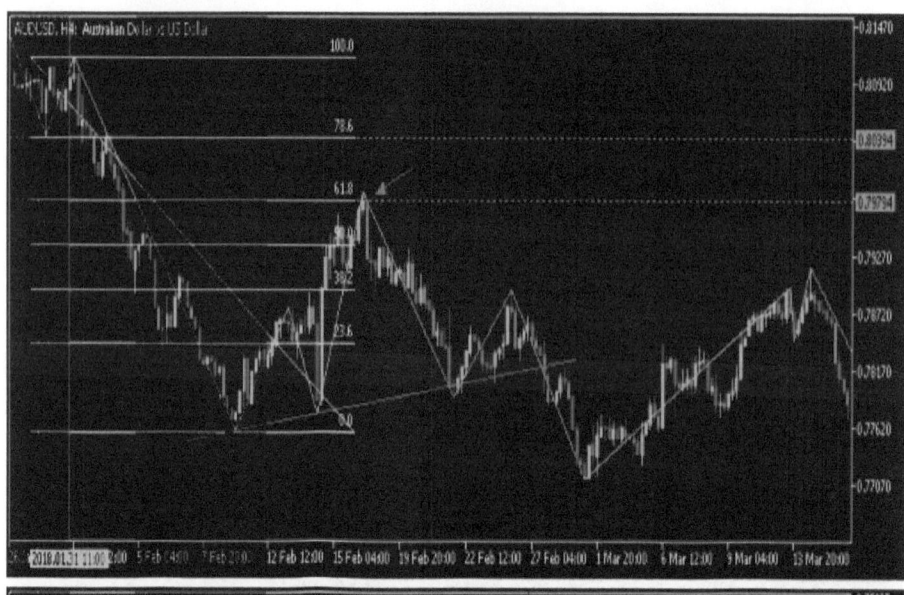
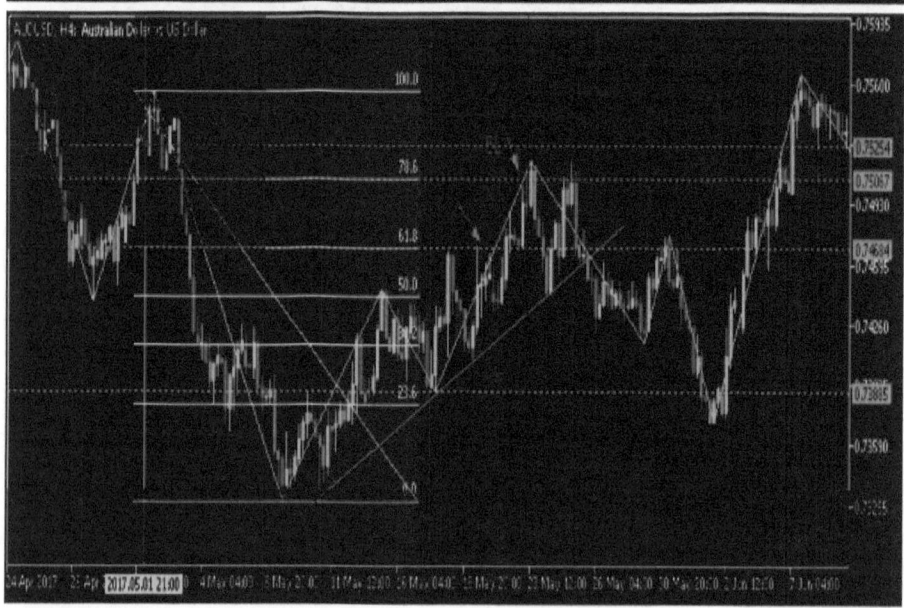

TECHNICAL ANALYSIS FOR FOREX DUMMIES

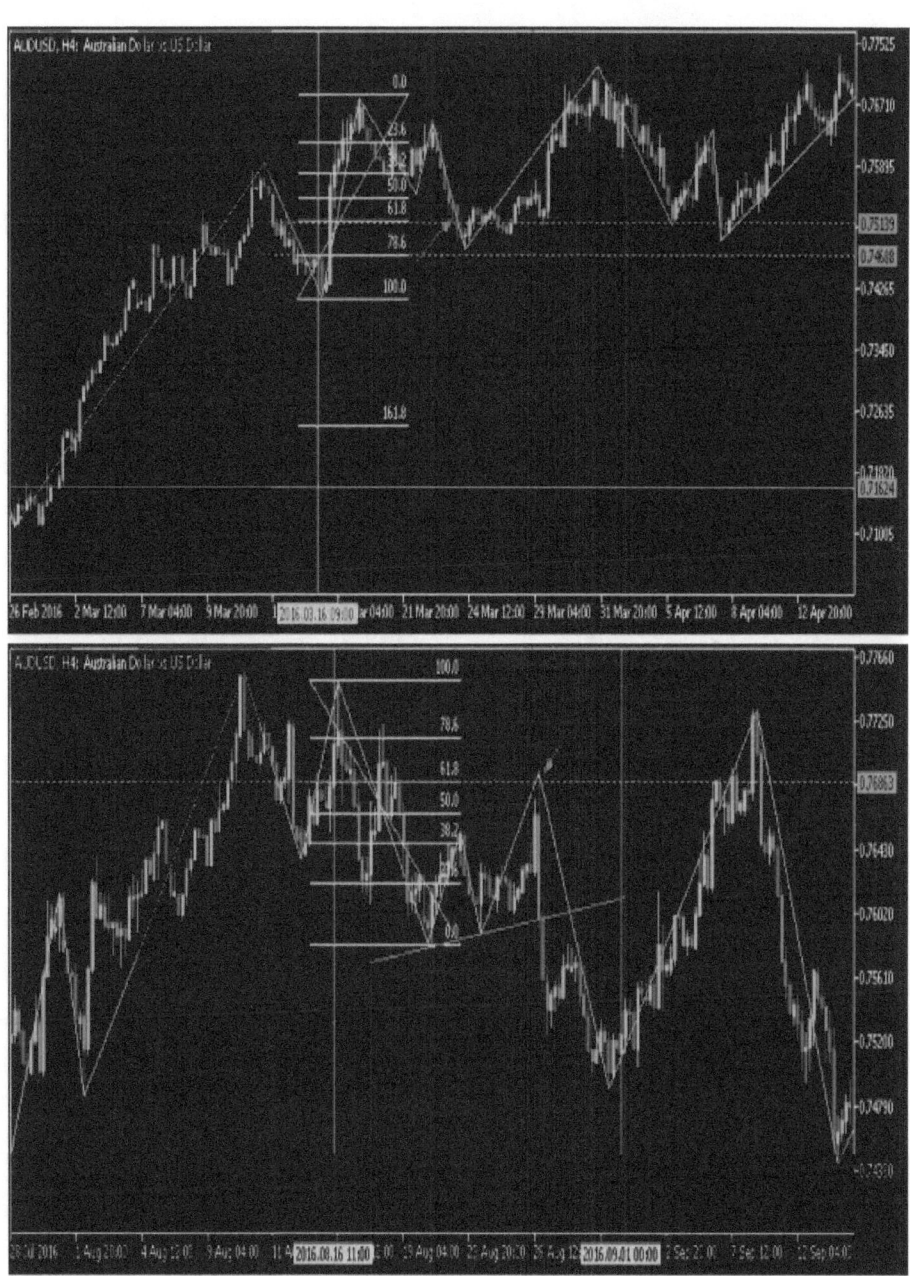

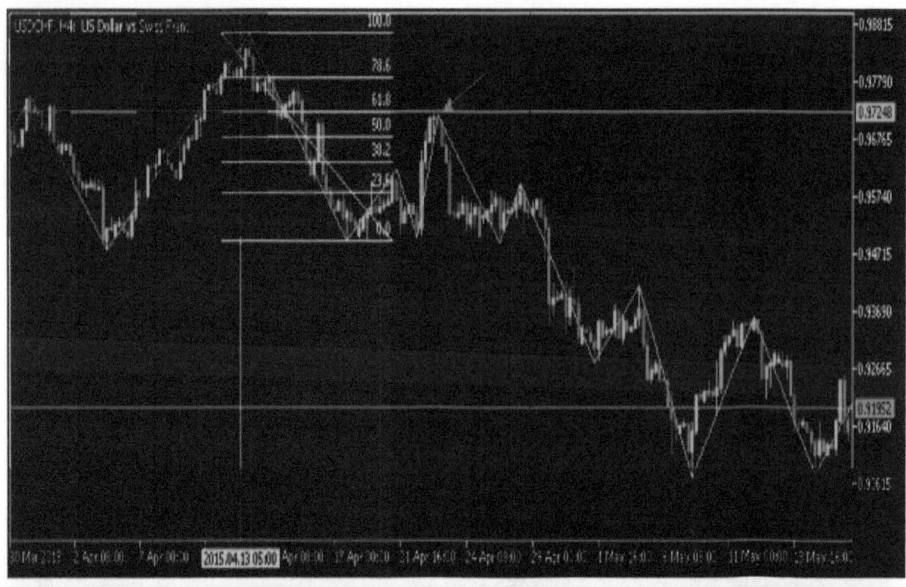

TECHNICAL ANALYSIS FOR FOREX DUMMIES

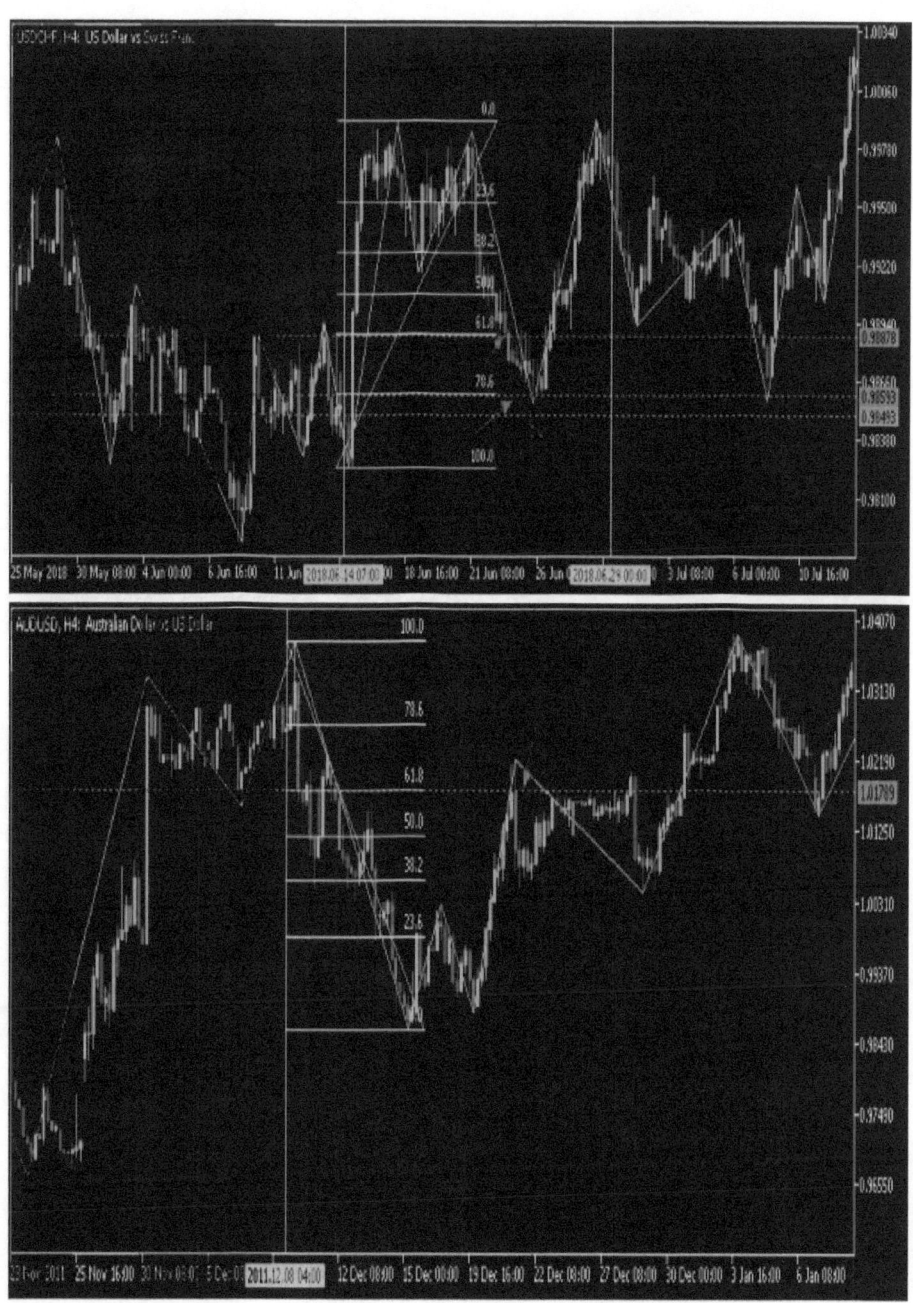

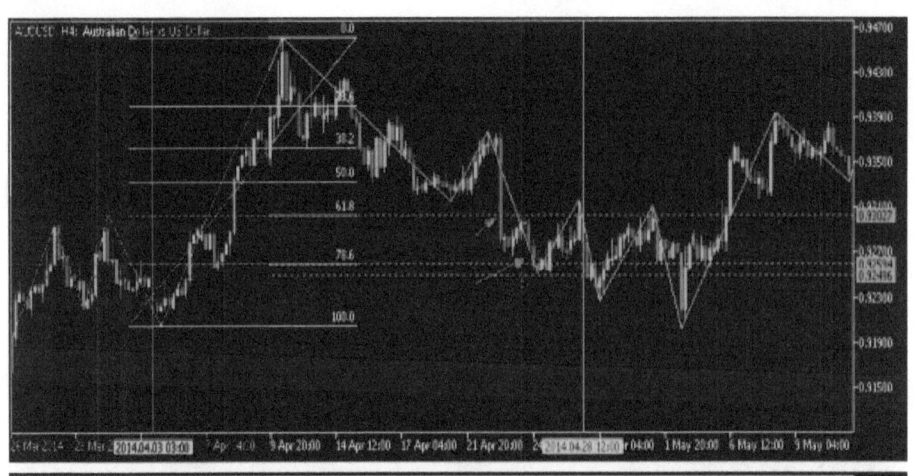

www.ingramcontent.com/pod-product-compliance
Lightning Source LLC
Chambersburg PA
CBHW030555220526
45463CB00007B/3086